PISA

monuments, works of art of the Cathedral and of the city

COMPLETE GUIDE
FOR VISITING THE CITY
with particular attention to the monuments in
PIAZZA DEI MIRACOLI

D0189701

edizioni **ITALCARDS**
bologna - italy

Distributore esclusivo
LA TORRE - Pisa

THE TOWN TODAY
ITS ORIGINS - ITS HISTORY

Pisa is divided in two parts by the Arno River. It is at 4 mts above sea-level and located on a fertile plain that extends from the foot of Pisa mountains to the sea-coast: which is 10 kms away from the towncenter. With a population just over one hundred thousand inhabitants Pisa has a military and civil international airport, is an archiepiscopal seat and also boasts a university centre of ancient historical and cultural traditions. The university of Pisa, in fact, has been attended since the twelfth century and is, therefore, one of the oldest, and most glorious, Italian universities. Pisa is also a main station on the Rome-Genoa railway line with branches to Empoli-Florence and Siena, as well as, on another line, to Lucca-Montecatini Terme-Florence. It is a junction of main and tollroads. That is the reason why from the town the numerous resorts on the Tyrrhenian Sea and in the mountains are easily accessible. Also the centres for thermal cures are included within an easy reach: S. Giuliano Terme at only 4 kms, Montecatini and Monsummano Terme at not more than 38-45 kms.

Regarding the climate, Pisa can be classified within the most temperate zones of Italy, because the Pisa mountains, the mountains of «Garfagnana» and the Apuanian Alps shelter it from the cold north winds, while the nearby seafront allows it to breathe the temperate west and south winds. As such the town is suitable for a pleasant stay, backed up by a first rate hotel organization and by the opportunity of having within a short range the many spots above mentioned besides other such as Lucca, Torre del Lago Puccini (with the country-house of the great composer), Collodi with its historical garden, Leghorn, etc., for rich experiences and

1. The assault and capture of Bona by Jacopo da Empoli, one of the six sections of the rich lacunar ceiling in the Church of S. Stefano dei Cavalieri, where the glorious deeds of the Knights are commemorated.

pleasure trips.

But the town is principally glorified for its ancient and noble past; it is said that Pisa is older than Rome and that is was one of the most powerful marine Republics.

Opinions about its origin are discordant: most likely it rose between the 5th and the 7th century B.C. At first it was a Greek colony, after an Etruscan one. From 180 B.C. it became a Roman colony named «Colonia Julia Pisana». The fortune of the town was always governed by the sea, that in this period was at the gates of Pisa. From the 11th century Pisa became a powerful marine Republic. That is to say after the period where it was allied with the Romans up to the second Punic war and afterwards when Caesar Octavian established the harbour in a natural bay (the «Sinus Pisanus») and precisely at the estuary of the Arno River where big ships could dock. Up to that time, it had been under Odoacer, the Ostrogothics, the Bizantines, the Longobards and the Franks, then annexed in the Marquisate of Tuscany under the Carolingians.

As a powerful marine Republic, Pisa fought against the Saracens and conquered Corsica, Sardinia and the Balearic Islands; it asserted its high prestige also in the East especially after having participated to the 1st Crusade. The problem now was to consolidate and to maintain its influence over the conquered territories and in this intention long and fierce struggles against Amalfi and Genoa for supremacy over lands and sea were never lacking. Added to this constant military effort there was strong internal unrests mainly caused by the Guelf-Tuscan league on account of speculations, of contrasts on how the enormous amassed wealth was to be administrated. The result was, that even though they managed to resist the Guelf-Free cities and the followers of Guelf, amongst the citizens of Pisa, the town became slowly weaker, so much so that being engaged contemporaneously, on the seas of Levant, in rivalry with the Republic of Venice, and on the Mediterranean against Genoa, it suffered a disastrous defeat by Genoa in the famous battle of Meloria in 1824. It was the «day of Saint Sistus» anniversary of many victories, but this time Pisa had lost. The Republic went on, but the glory, prestige and rule of the sea came to an end. In this manner, after an extraordinary adventure, the economical and political decline of Pisa started; the free-city institutes broke down and in their place the families of nobles asserted their authority: first came Uguccione della Faggiola, then the della Gherardesca and after the family Gambacorta. Finally the family D'Appiano ruled over the fortune of Pisa until it passed over to Visconti, that ceded it to the authority of Florence in the year 1405.

Although Pisa had now lost its political independence, nevertheless, under the wise rule of Medici, the town developed as a cultural and intellectual centre. Cosimo I de' Medici, for instance, renewed the study of the

Sapienza. Leopoldo the 2nd reorganized the Scuola Normale Superiore founded by Napoleon in the year 1810.

After so many historical vicissitudes, in the year 1860, Pisa joined the Kingdom of Italy with a solemn plebiscite.

During the 2nd World War the town was subjected to notable destructions from heavy bombing raids and because of the dogged resistance of the Germans on the northern banks of the Arno River, just within the limits of town-walls. This resistance lasted 40 days. Casualties were very high and the destruction was not limited to public property but also to artistic treasures. In the field of art the famous «Camposanto Monumentale» (Monumental churchyard), the marble walls of which close off the northern side of the imposing «Piazza dei Miracoli», was seriously damaged.

ARTISTIC OUTLINE THE GREAT CITIZENS OF PISA

In the field of architecture and in that of sculpture Pisa originated the so called «Pisa Romanic Style». The art so highly conceived and expressed opened its great chapter with the architect Buschetto in the 11th century. Then came RAINALDO, in the 13th century, to carry on the work begun by the first, who started the façade of the Cathedral. DIOTISALVI began, in his turn, the grandiose Baptistry in the 12th century. Later BONANNO PISANO started the construction of the Leaning Tower and at a certain moment works ceased, to remain untouched for 90 years. Afterwards came GIOVANNI DI SIMONE, who built other stores on the same style as the originator of this grandiose architectural work and about the middle of the 14th century, TOMMASO, son of ANDREA PISANO, finished the tower with the construction of the belfry. In these masterpieces of art, constructed during the period of major economical prosperity because of the marine enterprises of the Republic of Pisa, there is a wonderful combination of Romanesque, Mussulman and Gothic architecture to shape a new style, called «Pisa Romanic Style».

Not only the architecture but also the sculpture of Pisa was grandiose. The names of GUGLIELMO, BONANNO, NICOLA and GIOVANNI, his son, ANDREA, NINO, TOMMASO, are sufficient for indicating the high level of this grandiose art. The masterpieces of this group can be favourably compared to the works of the masters.

1 2

6

3

GALILEO GALILEI, FIBONAC-
CI, ANTONIO PACINOTTI, ULISSE
DINI were all citizens of Pisa. These
names alone are sufficient to establish
the proud and great tradition of the
town, together with its famous and ancient university.

In the field of painting Pisa takes a
place considerably inferior to that oc-
cupied in architecture and sculpture.
However, even if names of most promi-
nent artists are lacking, there is no reason to overlook the names of GIUN-
TA DA PISA, the brothers TEDICE
and the brothers VANNI, FRANCES-
CO TRAINI, CECCO DI PIETRO,
AURELIO LOMI, ORAZIO RIMI-
NALDI, G.B. TEMPESTI, MELANI
and others.

*1. Portrait of Galileo Galilei by Sustermans;
2. Galileo's birth certificate; 3. A view of
Piazza del Duomo (Cathedral Square) from
the ancient «Porta Nuova» (New Gate).*

7

CATHEDRAL SQUARE

The monuments which transform a common name of square into the «Piazza dei Miracoli» are: the CATHEDRAL, the BAPTISTRY, the BELL or LEANING TOWER and the MONUMENTAL CHURCHYARD. A combination of works of architecture and sculpture which rise stately and austere, but at the same time refined and full of charm, placed around a wide tender green lawn. It is in this natural simplicity that the white marbles, so highly worked and rendered precious by human genius, have found a perfect setting. It is exactly in this pleasant simplicity of the «LAWN» that the greatness of the works, seems almost a creation of nature itself, wonderfully blended, so much so that the tourist, even if passing hastily by, can't help but feel a strong sense of admiration and emotion. This wonderful architectural composition, with so much harmony of styles and colours, contrasts with the beauty of the ancient walls facing west and east, as well as the buildings of the 13th century facing south, today seat of the «Spedali Riuniti di S. Chiara».

The imposing magnificence of the marbles, the green of the lawn, the ancient walls with their embattlements, the sombre and solemn row of cypresses, form a whole really great, even touching play of lights at every hour of the day.

In the evening the sight is perhaps even more beautiful because as the sun sets a dim and soft illumination substitues its light, rendering the play of lights more suggestive and penetrating.

THE LEANING TOWER

History. This is the monument that, among the others of the «Piazza dei Miracoli», stirs the imagination of

A panoramic view of the city; 2. A view of the Tower from the cloister inside the Museum of the Opera del Duomo.

2 ▶

everybody, from the old to the young. Firstly we like to give you some information and events regarding its long history.

The construction of this imposing mass was started in the year 1174 by BONANNO PISANO. When the tower had reached its third storey the works ceased because it had started sinking into the ground. The tower remained thus for 90 years. It was completed by GIOVANNI DI SIMONE, TOMMASO, son of ANDREA PISANO, crowned the tower with the belfry at half of 14th century.

The top of the Leaning Tower can be reached by mounting the 294 steps which rise in the form of a spiral on the inner side of the tower walls.

The tower is 55.863 mts high.

The inside diameter at the base is 7.368 mts.

The outer diameter on the base is 15.484 mts.

There are 8 storeys.

It is supported by foundations of less than 3 mts.

The Tower weighs about 14,500 tons.

In the belfry there are 7 bells each one of them corresponding to a note of the musical scale.

The oldest bell is that named «Pasquareccia» which rang to announce that the Count Ugolino della Gherardesca, sentenced for treachery,

1. A remarkable Romanesque capital at the base of the leaning Tower; 2. Basso-rilievo at the base of the Tower showing the starting date of the building works; 3. The leaning Tower by Bonanno Pisano (1174) and the Putti Fountain by G. Vacca (18th century); at page 12-13 an aerial view of the monuments.

was starving to death together with his sons and nephews in the tower of Piazza delle Sette Vie (today Piazza dei Cavalieri). On the top of the tower GALILEO GALILEI carried out famous experiments regarding the effects of gravity. From the top we can enjoy a vast view, that starting from the Monte Pisano, the mountains of Garfagnana and the Apuanian Alps slopes down towards us, demonstrating the great extent of the whole fertile plain, which, before reaching the sea, meets the grandiose and extensive forest regions of Migliarino and S. Rossore.

Art. This very famous work is of Romanesque style, and as already stated dates back to the year 1174. Cylindrical in shape it is supplied with six open galleries. A cornice separates these galleries one from the other and each presents a series of small arches fitted on the capitals of the slender columns. In the base there is a series of big blind arcades with geometrical decorations. In the belfry there is the same design of arcades as that of the base, with the difference that here, there are, apart from the reduced proportions, the housings of the bells.

Although stately, this monument is not lacking in elegance and lightness due to the arcades and open galleries between one storey and another.

Although it can be considered a real masterpiece of architecture, this monument is mostly famous for its strong inclination. Regarding this inclination it can be safely stated that it is undoubtedly due to a sinking of the ground right from the time of its construction. Therefore, the assumption of those who desire to imagine that great tower was built inclined is entirely without foundation. Unfortunately, even today the great mass continues to sink very slowly. It is a question of about 1 mm. every year. Since nobody can state with mathematical security that this sinking will continue in the future at the present yearly rate, without its ceasing, remedies by means of adequate measures, based on scientific studies and projects, are under consideration. In the meantime supervision with instruments of very high precision is continously being carried out.

THE CATHEDRAL

This grandiose masterpiece of Romanesque-Pisa Style was started in the year 1063 by the great architect BUSCHETTO. It is, therefore, the first work undertaken in the spot that became later the «Piazza dei Miracoli». It was possible because of the enormous wealth amassed by the powerful Sea Republic which at that time Pisa was, particularly after a successful excursion on Palermo. The Cathedral was consecrated in the year 1118, even though still incomplete, by Pope Gelasio the 2nd. It was terminated in the 13th century, with the erection of the façade, unchanged up to today, by RAINALDO.

The Cathedral, designed in Latin-Cruciform, basically has a romanesque architectural style, but at the same time interpretes and absorbs elements of various styles, forming thus a unique style which has something of sublime. The Cathedral was adorned through the years with numerous works of art. GIOVANNI PISANO is certainly the artist who excels in these works, especially because he has given us the famous, extremely rich and ingenious PERGAMO (Pulpit).

For a brief idea of its dimensions, the Cathedral is about one hundred meters long and 54 meters high. The façade is 35.40 mts wide. It is 34.20 mts high, hence both imposing and of an ingenious and grandiose conception.

The façade of the cathedral is articulated in five orders of arches, the inferior of which has seven blind arches; the two lateral gates, and one central gate, are separated by columns and pilasters. In the year 1595 a furious fire broke out and destroyed these gates (as well as the ceiling and other works inside) hence the gates of today are not the original ones of BONANNO, but those made by the artists of the school of Giambologna, i. e. Francavilla, Mocchi, Tacca.

In the central gate is depicted the life of «Maria». The two lateral ones represent the life of the Redeemer. In this inferior order the walls show numerous tarsia-rose-windows, groves, inlays of ornamental glass, geometrical panels giving a sense of grace and

refinement.

The superior orders present open-galleries that contrast with the walls giving depth and movement so much so that the massive proportions of the whole façade become refined; at the same time, they are rendered precious by a minute and elaborate fretwork.

Above the central gate, there is a memorial inscription of Rainaldo. The sarcophagus of BUSCHETTO, who started the construction of the cathedral, lays in the first arcade to the left. On the top of the façade, there is a statue of the Madonna of Andrea Pisano and at the sides angels of the School of Giovanni Pisano. At both sides of the first order of galleries there

1

2

are the statues of two evangelists. The whole cathedral, both on the two sides and on the parts of the apses, repeats the decorative and ornamental themes of the façade, even if with slight differences. Also here, decorations are repeated well as polychrome-tarsias, groved panels, inlays of coloured glass. The whole cathedral is a wonderful work of architecture and sculpture not at all lacking in grace in spite of its stately and massive conception.

The oval shaped dome shows influences of Islamic art and is located at the intersection of the transept with the central body of the temple.

The gate of St. Ranieri, with its

1. A view of the Cathedral dome from the Tower; 2. The Cathedral apse; 3. The central door of the Cathedral with the history of Mary's life.

16

3 ▶

To read panels, follow this order: start on the first column of the left-hand wing of the door, from top to bottom. Then, in the same order, pass on to the second column. Then turn to the right-hand wing from top to bottom, starting on the third column, and ending with the fourth.

bronze pillars built by BONANNO PISANO, is a masterpiece of art that shows traces of Byzantine influences. It was built in the year 1180, and made up of 24 panels whereon are represented the «History of the Redeemer's life». On the outside of the gate, there is a lunette with «the Madonna, the Infant and two Angels», work relief of Andrea di Francesco GUARDI.

Inside of the cathedral visit to the works of art. In order to enjoy all the majesty of the temple, before stopping here and there, we advise you to stop near the inner will of the cathedral façade. From here the view is total and its effect is such to convey a deep religion feeling. To this feeling is added a sense of bewilderment, as we stand before the vastness and profoundity of every architectural and sculptural work, as if not the hand of the man but a divine wall had aimed at creating what we are admiring. If we place ourselves in the middle of the nave, near the inner wall of the cathedral, our attention will be drawn to the long line of the imposing granite colonnades, which are almost all antique and have capitals of Corinthian style. Then the women's gallery with little loggias lo-

cated above the nave, the rich, highly decorated lacunar ceiling, the ample, profound, terminal apse whereon Christ on his throne contrasts, will complete our admiration.

In brief everything including the play of the minor colonnades, the black and white panels, which line the walls, helps to give vivacity and movement to the grandiose realization of the temple.

Let us now pass to its description and to the visit. Internally it is divided into five aisles, one central major aisle and the minor ones two on each side. The transept has three aisles. Against the second line of columns of the central nave there are two holy water founts. The statues thereon are, on one side, Jesus and on the other side St. John the Baptist (17th century, of F. Palma).

Right aisle. On the inner wall of the façade, looking towards the right aisle, there is the tomb of Matteo Rinuccini, over which hangs a bronze «Crucifix» of the 17th century, of Pietro Tacca. Along the long righthand wall there are four altars of STAGIO STAGI with paints of some artists of the 17th and 18th century, such as CAVALLUCCI, TEMPESTI, CONCA, BEZZUOLI and others. Furthermore, there are in-

The door called «Porta di San Ranieri» by Bonanno Pisano (1180)

LEFT WING		RIGHT WING	
Panel No. 1	Christ in the Glory among the Angels	Panel No. 13	The assumption of the Virgin among the Angels
Panel No. 2	The descent into Limbo	Panel No. 14	The ascension
Panel No. 3	The maundy	Panel No. 15	Judas' kiss
Panel No. 4	Jesus in the desert tempted by the devil	Panel No. 16	The resurrection of Lazarus
Panel No. 5	The presentation in the temple	Panel No. 17	The slaughter of the innocents
Panel No. 6	The annunciation	Panel No. 18	The nativity
Panel No. 7	The resurrection	Panel No. 19	The death of Mary
Panel No. 8	The last supper	Panel No. 20	The crucifixion
Panel No. 9	The transfiguration	Panel No. 21	The entry into Jerusalem
Panel No. 10	The flight into Egypt	Panel No. 22	The baptism of Jesus
Panel No. 11	Mary visiting St. Elizabeth	Panel No. 23	The adoration of the Magi
Panel No. 12	Prophets under the palm trees	Panel No. 24	Prophets under the palm trees

5

4

Bronze panels of the S. Ranieri Door by Bonanno Pisano. *1. The slaughter of the innocents; 2. The nativity; 3. The baptism of Jesus; 4. The adoration of the Magi; 5. The Annunciation; 6. The Cathedral nave.*

6 ▶

laid seats of G. da Maiano and other artists.

At the 1st altar there is «The Virgin in her glory», of C. Allori, also named Bronzino.

At the 2nd altar «the dispute on the sacrament», of F. Vanni.

At the 3rd altar «The Madonna of the Graces», of Andrea del Sarto and G.A. Sogliani.

At the 4th altar there is a marble urn dominated by a lunette with a sculpture representing God the Father, work of B. Ammannati.

We are now at the right arm of the transept and turning towards we immediately see an altar with «Madonna sitting on a throne and Saints» made by Pierin del Vaga and G.A. Sogliani. Still further along the walls there are two large paintings of the 18th century. At the end of the arm in the centre there is the Chapel of St. Ranieri, work of architect B. Lorenzi. The sculptures are of the same author, see the statue of St. Efisio, as well as of F. Mosca, Stoldo Lorenzi, P. Guidotti. In the apse there is a 14th century mosaic, subjected to notable restauration, representing the «Madonna in her Glory».

On the opposite side of the transept, i. e. on the left hand wall facing the apse, we find the sarcophagus of the Emperor of Luxemburg Henry VII. This is a very valuable work of Tino da Camaino. A part of this tomb is missing and it is kept in the Museum of the «Opera del Duomo»: it depicts the figures of the Counsellors. Immediately beyond the St. Ranieri Gate there is an altar of Stagio Stagi and P. Fancelli with the central sculpture of «St. Biagio». Practically in front of this altar there is a holy water fount with a statue of the «Madonna with Infant», a work of Rossimino.

The presbytery is surrounded by a balustrade on which there are two bronze angels of GIAMBOLOGNA and his pupils. Inside there are the remains of the ancient choral hall, that was almost completely destroyed with other works by the famous fire in the year 1595. Here, we can admire two famous paintings situated at the two pillars: the one on the right, facing the altar, is «St. Agnes» of Andrea del Sarto, to the left is the «Madonna with Infant» of G. Sogliani.

In the two chancels there are four extremely beautiful paintings of Andrea del Sarto: «St. Catherine» and «St. Margaret» to the right and to the left «St. Peter» and «St. John the Baptist».

On the high altar there is a bronze crucifix of GIAMBOLOGNA. Furthermore, there are six angels, a work of L. POGLIAGHI. Following the APSE, where, at the entrance, we find frescoes of M. CINGANELLI and an «Angels Musicians» of GHIRLANDAIO. This later work has been repainted over the original version.

High in the basin of the apse there is a large mosaic depicting «The Redeemer between the Blessed Virgin and St. John» to which realization also CIMABUE cooperated. Many works decorate the whole apse behind the High Altar. There are paintings of Beccafumi such as «St. Matthew and St. Mark», others depicting scenes from the Bible and of Moses breaking the Tables of the Law. Furthermore, there are works of Sogliani and Sodoma among which «The Deposition from the Cross», «The Sacrifice of Abraham», «St. Luke and St. John».

Other paintings are of R. Manetti, M. Rosselli, P. Guidotti, A. Lomi, O. Riminaldi.

Left transept. On leaving the Presbytery we can immediately enter the left transept where, along the right aisle, we find the «Tomb of the Archbishop of Elci», of G.B. Vacca and paintings of P. Sorri, A. Lomi, D. Passignano. Also

1. Cathedral presbytery, high altar and apse with the great mosaic started by Francesco De Simone and finished by Cimabue, showing Jesus the Almighty between the Virgin and St. John.

2

1. The urn of S. Ranieri by G.B. Foggini (1688); 2. Sepulchral monument of the Emperor Arrigo VII of Luxembourg, by Tino da Camaino; 3. Virgin and Child by A. Sogliani.

3

*1. S. Agnese by Andrea del Sarto; 2. The
lamp of Galileo Galilei.*

to be noted is a 15th century white marble holy water fount of G. da Milano.

At the arm end, is the «Chapel of the Holy Sacrament», a work of B. Lorenzi. Here the sculptures are of F. Mosca (16th century). The altar and the bronze ciborium with silver parts are of G.B. Foggini (17th century). At the sides of the altar, in two niches, we see to the left «St. Mary Magdalene» and to the right «St. Christine» (C. Fancelli). In the basin of the apse there is a mosaic of the 14th century showing «The Annunciation». On continuing the visit and passing to the left wall of the transept we see other paintings of the same authors as on the right wall. At the end of this wall there is a marble altar of Stagio Stagi.

Left aisle. Round the corner, after having visited the left arm of the transept, we enter directly into the main body of the Church, i. e. into the left aisle. Going towards the façade, we find the first of the four altars of Stagio Stagi and in a lunette of this work we see the picture of «The Apparition of the Virgin to St. Ranieri» (B. Lorenzi). Continuing in the same direction in the following marble altars: «God in His Glory» of V. Salimbeni, the «Holy Ghost and Martyrs» of D. Passignano and «The Crucifix and the Saints» of G.B. Paggi.

Also in this aisle of the temple main body, as in the right one already visited, there are paintings of the 18th century and inlaid seats among the altars.

At this point, very little remains to be done but to go to the center of the Cathedral to admire THE PULPIT, THE DOME, THE LAMP OF GALILEO. Before speaking of the pulpit, which is described in a separate chapter, we wish to give the following pointers:

The lamp of Galileo is in the middle of the church. It is a bronze chandelier commonly called the «Lamp of Galileo» following a popular tradition, according to which the great citizen of Pisa Galileo Galilei on observing the obscillations of the pendant, established the isochronism of the obscillations of the pendulum. However, the fact remains that this chandelier is a fine work realized in the year 1587.

The dome is above the right arm of the transept and is supported by imposing peak arches inspired by the Arabian-Muslam Style. It is ellipsoidal shaped. On the vault there is a frescoe of Orazio Riminaldi representing the «Assumption».

The pulpit. We are before a work of rare richness if not one of the greatest masterpieces. In this work the plasticity of the representation seems animated of sensibility and tension that's nearly dramatic.

Nicola Pisano, father of Giovanni, in his Pulpit in the Baptistry, for instance, expresses himself with a religious gravity peculiar to works of the Romanesque period. His son Giovanni in his work in the Cathedral, which we are now dealing with, has on the contrary completely renounced to this precise and calculated reproduction, giving breath and outlet to a vehement

2

vivacity and to a deep human sense which comes to light from his figures.

The pulpit with its hexagonal base, work of Giovanni Pisano (1302-1310), is located near the first pillar of the vault. In the year 1599 it was dismantled and rebuilt only in the year 1926. It rests on eleven columnar supports that in turn rest respectively on lions and on pedestals. Other supports are represented by the statues of St. Michael, Hercules, the Evangelists supporting Christ and «The four Cardinal virtues» which, in turn, support the Church. The central one represents «The Arts of the Trivium and Quadrivium». The capitals of the supports are sculptured with figures of Sibyls. In the lateral corbels there are Evangelists and Prophets. A cornice separates the above illustrated portion from the panels composing the upper portion of

the pulpit and the figures of Prophets
and Saints that are located between the
panels. In the panels the events preceed-
ing and following Christ's birth are dra-
matically represented. They are:

1) Annunciation - Visitation - Birth of
   St. John the Baptist.
2) Birth of Jesus Christ.
3) The Wise Kings.
4) Presentation at the temple and the
   flight into Egypt.
5) The slaughter of the innocents.
6) The kiss of Judas - The arrest of
   Christ - The scourging of Christ.
7) The Crucifixion.
8) The chosen ones.
9) The reprobates.

At this point the visit is finished and
it only remains to glance once more
around the whole temple and then to
go out into the vast lawn «of the mira-
cles».

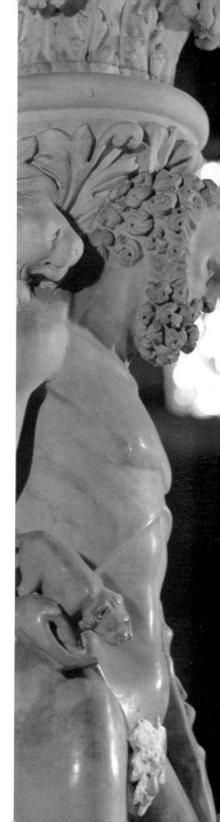

*1. The pulpit by Giovanni Pisano; 2. Her-
cules' nude with the club in his left hand.*

The Cathedral pulpit. *1. Famous group of the four cardinal virtues: the «Justice» with the scales and the sword, the «Temperance» holding the cornucopia and the compass in her hand, the «Fortitude» sustaining the lion by the legs, and the «Prudence» nude.*

Above the group, the «Church», represent ed by a woman suckling two children, prob ably the Old and New Testament; 2. Pane with the crucifixion; 3. Panel with the slaughter of the innocents.

2

3

4

THE BAPTISTRY

It is located in front of the cathedral façade. The construction of this great building began in the year 1153 under the guide of the architect DIOTISAL-VI, as stated on an epigraph situated inside the monument on a pillar. Hence it was the second monument to rise in the square, given that the works of the church bell-tower (or Leaning Tower) began many years later, i. e. in the year 1174. Also in the case of the Baptistry,

as for the other monument of the «Piazza dei Miracoli», from the beginning to the end of the works many years lapsed with interruptions due to different causes. In fact, only at the end of the 14th century the work was terminated.

The Baptistry has a circular base, presents three orders (or stories) and from the third order (or Tambour) rises the dome. The height of this imposing monument is 55 mts, with a diameter of 35.50 mts. It has four gates, the principal of which opens towards the façade of the Cathedral. In spite of its gigantic mass, its aspect is refined by a multiple series of ornaments in Gothic style. The first storey is with blind arcades like the Leaning Tower and the Cathedral, but windows have one light. The second order or storey presents an open gallery surmounted by ornamental aedicules with «busts». There are, furthermore, cusps, on which rest statues of Nicola PISANO and of his school. Such sculptures which, as we have said, are both in the niches and in the cusps of this second storey, are

1. The Baptistry, the building of which started in 1153 and finished in 1500; 2. The architrave of the entrance door; 3. The door left jamb: a detail of the months; 4. The entrance door lunette with a copy of the Madonna by G. Pisano. The original lies inside the Museum of the Opera del Duomo.

in the most part substituted by copies, while the originals are at the Museum of the «Opera del Duomo». Other cusps magnificently rise, between the aedicules and minor cusps, extending beyond the second order or storey, up to the third order (or tambour), at the same height of the extremely beatiful mullioned windows with two lights which are the main ornament of this storey. Above the third order or storey rises the dome whereon there are other windows between the ribs. Regarding the «Entrance Gate» which is in front of the Cathedral façade we will simply list the art represented on this great portal. Here are the sculptures of a unknown author of the 13th century. On the right hand-post are depicted in relief «The Apostles», «The Descent into Hell» and «David». On the left hand-post are represented «The Months of the Year». The two fillet-architrave presents on the upper part «Jesus between the Virgin and the Baptist, Angels and Evangelists». On the inferior part there is «The History of the Baptist». Above the architrave opens a lunette, that in its centre depicts a copy of the Madonna of Giovanni Pisano. The original of this Madonna of the great master is in the Museum of the «Opera del Duomo». In the sculptured under-arch of the lunette there are shown «The Agnus Dei» and «The 24 Seniors». Also the other portal that faces the walls of the «Churchyard» is magnificently decorated. In the architrave there is a sculpture with «The Annunciation and Saints».

Baptistry: inside. On entering the baptistry, the immensity of the building is even more convincing than from outside. Here, in fact, we obtain an immediate sense of the proportions. We have stated that the height is 55 mts and the diameter 35.50 mts: bare values, but from the inside, at this moment, the height and amplitude have another meaning, so penetrating as to cause admiration and dismay. We are, in fact, under the huge vault of the dome and in front of a grandiose annular nave discreetly lighted by the numerous windows distributed all around. We are facing an imposing and high colonnade alternated with pillars that detached from the wall, delimitate a nave. Above is a very wide gallery with high arcades well lighted by windows.

Inside of the Baptistry: Font. Our attention will be very soon drawn by the Font and the Pulpit. The font is located in the middle of the temple on three steps. It is a work of the 13th century of GUIDO BIGARELLI. The big octagonal basin, which incorporates other four smaller basins, was realized for baptism by immersion. In the middle of the basin there is a statue of the Baptist, of ITALO GRISELLI. The font is enriched with eight faces decorated by central rose-windows and by geometrical marble decorations. The al-

2

tar, located close to the font is composed of six panels with marble inlays and rose-windows. It is surrounded by inlaid seats of the 17th century. Looking towards the altar we can appreciate a cosmati-floor of the 14th century.

Inside of the Baptistry: Pulpit. This is a great work of the year 1260 of NICOLA PISANO. The artist for realizing the last panel of this opera, took advantage of the work of his still very young son Giovanni and of ARNOLFO DI CAMBIO, both of which later, cooperated with him in realizing the pulpit for the cathedral of Siena. The pulpit of the baptistry has a hexagonal base supported by seven columns, three of which rest on supporting lions, on the sides. The central column rests on a base depicting sculptured animals and human figures. This work evidently reveals a marked inspiration of the artist to the romanesque art of his time and a need to express himself with a composed piety. Nevertheless it is not lacking in poetry even though it doesn't seem to exalt a human sense of inspiration, what on the contrary his son Giovanni did in the grandiose realization of the pulpit of the cathedral.

In the pendentives of the little arches there are figures of «Prophets». In the pillars of the corners are depicted: «Faith», «Charity», «Force», «Humility», «Fidelity» and «Innocence». In

Inside of the Baptistry. *1. Font by Guido da Como (1246); 2. One of the rosettes adorning the front of the Font.*

35

the panels there are represented:

1) The Nativity and Announcement to the Shepherds.
2) The Adoration of the Wise Kings.
3) The Presentation in the Temple.
4) The Crucifixion.
5) The Last Judgment.

Inside of the Baptistry. *1. The pulpit by Nicola Pisano who sculptured it between 1255 and 1260; 2. A panel of the pulpit showing the adoration of the Magi.*

◄ 1

2

1

In the baptistry if one asks the attendants, it is interesting to hear the echo. On the inside, for instance, a melody reechoes many times through the ample vault and gives the impression of hearing a strange, harmonious and multitoned big organ.

Inside of the Baptistry. *1. A panel of the pulpit showing the nativity; 2. Little trilobated arch with the figure of the Evangelist Matthew; 3. Inside of the Monumental Cemetery; 4. Entrance door of the Monumental Cemetery surmounted by the graceful Gothic decoration of the tabernacle. At page 40-41 inside of the Cemetery.*

THE CHURCHYARD

Outside. Coming out of the baptistry and looking once more at the majestic façade of the cathedral one will see to the left the churchyard which presents long marble walls in the form of a rectangle. These boundary walls are composed of blind-arcades on pilasters similar to those of the cathedral, tower and baptistry just visited. In these walls there are two entrances in the arcades. The main gate is on the right to the cathedral, over which stands out a Gothic three-cusped tabernacle with «Madonna and Saints». It is a work of the school of Giovanni Pisano.

Before passing over to other descriptions it is to be said that the churchyard dates back to about the end of the 13th century and was started by GIOVANNI DI SIMONE. Centuries passed before it was ultimated, just as for the other monuments of the square.

It is said that the archbishop Ubaldo de' Lanfranchi, in 1200, brought earth from the Golgotha Mountain with galleys coming back from a crusade, because it seems that this earth was capable of reducing a body into a skeleton within twenty four hours.

39

When Giovanni di Simone started the works the churchyard already existed. In fact, his aim in beginning this monumental work, was to gather in an orderly and dignified manner within a limited area all the graves scattered around the cathedral and at the same time to leave space for others in the future as was the custom in the noble families of Pisa.

Later, ancient sculptures, sepulchral monuments, works of art scattered around the city, were gathered inside the churchyard. Sarcofagi of famous men lined up against the walls, that were frescoed by great artists. Thus the «Camposanto Monumentale» (Monumental churchyard) of Pisa progressively became one of the greatest and richest galleries of medieval painting and sculpture, besides representing a great masterpiece of architecture. During the 2nd World War this enormous artistic and cultural patrimony suffered severe damages and losses especially from the bombing raid of the 27th July 1944. The roof caught fire melting the lead-plates covering the roof and the molten lead dropped down on the works of art. Today many of these works have been restored but have not been situated in their original places and are temporarily scattered here and there around the walls. Others are located in special rooms.

The churchyard from inside - Visit to the works of art. On entering the churchyard one's attention is immediately drawn to the great colonnade that opens out on an inner lawn with its great, round arcades. These latter are each adorned by quadruple lancet windows with fine, plurilobed, little arches. Nevertheless, looking around at the walls of the colonnade and seeing only the remains of frescoes we can't but feel a deep sorrow in thinking what our eyes could have admired today if the rage of the 2nd World War had saved this monumental spot. Saddened by this thought now it remains to content oneself by imagining the precious art gallery as it was before the war and looking for the remaining works removed to be restored. For some of

these pieces, a special room has been arranged, collecting, among many, «The Triumph of the Death», «The Last Judgment», «The Anchorets». Concerning the sinopites (preparatory sketches of the frescoes, brought to light when the same frescoes were detached from the walls for restauration) it is to be said that they are of great interest and are collected in the Museum of Sinopites.

The principal works are:

Southern arm. (Here opens the main gate). Very interesting are two tables of

1. The Cemetery North Gallery after the fire of July 27th 1944; 2. The Cemetery North Gallery; 3. The chains of the Pisan port returned by the citizens of Florence and Genoa as a token of fraternity.

Western arm. Francesco Ferrucci da Fiesole is the author of the «Sepolcral Monument of the Jurisconsult Francesco Vegio». Also interesting are the remains of the tomb of Counts della Gherardesca (Tommaso Pisano) and many Roman sarcophagi of appreciable value.

North wall. There are many Roman and Greek sarcophagi, one of which, famous, was the grave of Beatrix di Canossa mother of the Countess Mathilda. On this sarcophagus is depicted the History of Hippolitus and Phaedra. In this room frescoes of Buonamico di Buffalmacco, such as «The Triumph of the Death».

Eastern arm. Here is the monumental tomb of Filippo Decio, a work of Stagio Stagi with the figure of the late jurist on the lid. Also here are Roman sarcophagi and tombs. Giovanni Dupré is the author of the monument of the scientist Ottaviano Fabrizio Mosotti.

the period when Pisa was a Roman colony. Observe also a fragment of a column, a piece of mosaic and many Roman sarcophagi. Nothing remains of the frescoes that were on these walls. Some of these, restored, are arranged in a special room, the entrance of which is in the opposite wall.

3

QVAMVIS PECCATRIX SVM DOMNA VOCATA BEATRIX
IN TVMVLO MESA IACEO QVAE COMITISSA.
A·D·M·LXXVI.

4

5

1. Fragment of a Greek grave stele (3rd century b.C.); 2. Neo-Attic marble vase showing a Bacchic procession (3rd century b.C.); 3. Roman tomb slab; 4. Sarcophagus showing the history of Hippolytus and Phaedra (2nd century); 5. A detail of the sarcophagus with histories of Hippolytus and Phaedra. At page 46-47 fresco of «The Triumph of Death».

47

THE MUSEUM OF THE SINOPITES

The museum has been set up in a time-battered hospital pavilion, restored in 1979, which was part of a building erected in 1257 by Giovanni di Simone, the same architect who, later on, would build the Monumental Cemetery. The historical link between these two constructions was to manifest itself again after centuries. In 1944 the Cemetery was devastated by a fire during which the works of art preserved in its rooms and, above all, the famous fresco cycle painted on its walls, were badly damaged. The following peeling off of the damaged frescoes, which was a necessary stage of the restoration, has brought to light the preparatory sketches which had been hidden by the plaster. The discovery of the sinopites, whose name comes from the Turkish town of Sinope which supplied the earth used as colouring matter to paint them, has been a major artistic event, both because these works had remained unseen up to that time and because, thanks to the freshness of their execution, they sometimes are more valuable than the corresponding frescoes. The fifty or so sketches displayed in the museum were painted on the walls of

the Camposanto in the 14th and 15th century and represent undoubtedly the biggest collection of its kind. The artists are those considered as the authors of the Camposanto frescoes: Buonamico di Buffalmacco, Francesco Traini, Antonio Veneziano, Spinello Aretino, Taddeo Gaddi, Piero di Puccio and Benozzo Gozzoli.

On the upper floors visitors walk on modern modular structures; photographic reproductions on panels of the most important frescoes allow comparisons which reveal the author's insights and changes of mind during the tormenting phases of the thinking up and execution of the paintings.

Finally, it is advisable to visit the Monumental Cemetery in order to complete the information acquired in the Museum of the Sinopites.

Museum opening times: 9 to 12.30 a.m. - 3 to 7 p.m. during the summer; 9 to 12.30 a.m. - 3 to 4.30 p.m. during the winter.

The change from the summer to the winter opening times occurs gradually, following the length of daylight.

1. Entrance front of the Museum of the sinopites; 2. Detail of the sinopite representing the Last Judgement; 3. Exposition room of the sinopites; 4. History of the anchorites: Panuntius and Abraham (detail).

49

THE MUSEUM OF THE CATHEDRAL VESTRY BOARD

The museum contains works which used to adorn the monuments of the Piazza dei Miracoli and which, mainly for safety reasons, had been moved to the warehouses of the Cathedral Vestry Board. It was set up in 1986 in a specially restored building, between Piazza dell'Arcivescovado and Piazza del Duomo, which had been originally designed as a capitular seat (13th century) and then turned into an enclosure monastery. The exhibition takes up rooms on two different floors and the visit is made pleasant by the variety of works displayed and by an exceptionally good set of captions.

On the ground floor the following works are of particular value: the wooden crucifix by Borgognone; the bronze hippogryph; the Citharoedus David; the Madonnas by Giovanni Pisano, particularly the so-called «Madonna del colloquio» and the ivory small statue; the sculptures by Tino di Camaino, by Nino and Tommaso Pisano, by Andrea Guardi, etc.; the precious objects forming the «Treasure», with the crucifix by Giovanni Pisano, the Limoges caskets and the «Cathedral's belt»; the silverware of the Cathedral sacristy. On the upper floor: large paintings on canvas; some of the Cathedral's old fittings together with some precious wooden marquetries; miniated parchments; sacred vestments; printings of the 19th century representing the frescoes of the Camposanto and a rich archeological collection with Roman, Etruscan and Egyptian ojects.

These works flow before visitors along the museum path, thus reminding them of the events which accompanied the life of the monuments and of the town of Pisa: the Islamic influences, the sculptures of the 14th century, the spiritual inheritance of the ancient Rome.

Museum opening times:
8 a.m. to 7.30 p.m. during the summer;
9 a.m. to 4.30 p.m. during the winter.

The change from the summer to the winter opening times occurs gradually, following the length of daylight.

1. Museum of the Opera del Duomo; 2. Portico with statues; 3. Cloister.

Inside of the Museum. *1. First room: marble tarsias and Burgundian Christ; 2. Islamic bronze sculpture of the hippogriff; 3. Fourth room: sculptures by G. Pisano; 4. Madonna and Child called «Madonna del Colloquio»; 5. Virgin and Child, an ivory sculpture by G. Pisano.*

PIAZZA DEI CAVALIERI

After the «Piazza dei Miracoli» we would suggest to start the visit of the town from the «Piazza dei Cavalieri» (Knights' square) not only because it is the most important and beautiful square, after that of the cathedral, but also because it is nearby. Leaving the cathedral and entering the old Via S. Maria and after along Via dei Mille, we come out at Piazza dei Cavalieri. We find here a group of buildings that surrounds it irregularly but at the same time with an extraordinary harmony. We notice at once the Palace of the Knights' Caravan (after which the

1. Palazzo dei Cavalieri (Knight's Palace); 2. Monument to Cosimo I de' Medici by Francavilla; 3. Church of S. Stefano dei Cavalieri.

square is named), and where now seats the «Scuola Normale Superiore». Beyond that, we see the National Church of St. Stephen of the Knights. The Clock Palace is on the left of the entrance of the Via dei Mille. On the opposite side of the Clock Palace, there is the Palace of Puteano College and the Council Palace of the Order of the Knights of St. Stephen. The fountain located in the square is a work of the year 1596 of P. Francavilla. In proximity to it is the statue of Cosimo the 1st de' Medici, who founded the Order of the Knights of St. Stephen in the year 1562.

NATIONAL CHURCH OF ST. STEPHEN OF THE KNIGHTS

This is an opera of the 16th century of Vasari who, later, built also the bell-tower in 1572. The church presents a

marble façade of Don Giovanni de' Medici (1606) with a single portal in the middle, above which is the Emblem of the Knights Order. Flanking the sides of the church are two wings that were once used as dressing-rooms for the knights of the order of St. Stephen. These are later transformed into two aisles of the church by Pier Francesco Silvani.

INSIDE is a nave with an extremely beautiful wooden inlaid ceiling. In each of the six partitions, into which it is divided, is a painting representing «The glory of the knights». These works are of C. Allori, Empoli, Ligozzi and Cigoli.

On entering the church we can admire two precious holy water founts of Vasari while, on the right and left hand walls, we see between the windows four ship lanterns. These same walls are hung with tapestries and flags captured from the Turks. In this church there are also figureheads of ships of the Order of St. Stephen. Still on the walls we see four distempers (two on each side) representing «Episodes of St. Stephen Life», works of Vasari, Empoli, Allori and Ligozzi. To be noted also is the small but precious marble pulpit of the year 1627 of C. Fancelli. The walls of the church have four doors — two on both sides — which open into the two aisles that, as already mentioned, were previously used as dressing-rooms for the Knights of St. Stephen.

In the right aisle at the first altar we see the «Lapidation of St. Stephen» of G. Vasari. At the second altar there is a crucifix of Tacca. In the left aisle at the first altar, near the exit of the church, there is «The miracle of the loaves and fishes» of Buti; at the second altar the «Nativity of Jesus» opera of Bronzino.

At the high altar there is the sarcophagus of St. Stephen Pope (P.F. Silvani and Giovan Battista Foggini, 1700). Behind the altar a gilt bronze bust of «St. Lussorio» of Donatello is preserved under a glass-bell.

Of the palaces which surround the square let us dwell a little upon the one that today is the seat of the «Scuola Normale Superiore», a renovation of

1

2

Vasari — 16th century — of the old Palace of the Elders of the Pisan Republic. This building was appointed by Cosimo I de' Medici to receive the military order of the Knights of St. Stephen, hence it was also called «PALACE OF THE CARAVAN». Observe the originality of the building, its slight curvature with a graffito-decorated façade, with a series of busts of the Grand Dukes of Tuscany of that time at the second storey and in the middle, above a balcony, the escutcheon of the Medici family.

Now we are in front of the original PALACE OF THE CLOCK that is a successful architectural utilization of two ancient TOWERS constructed from designs of VASARI, that is the tower of GUALANDI (or Gherardesca) with the other of the TOWN-JAIL or TORRE DELLE SETTE VIE. In the tower of Gualandi Count Ugolino della Gherardesca, imprisoned for treachery together with sons and nephews, starved to death. Count Ugolino was at that time Podestà of the town and the Marine Republic of Pisa had just suffered a clamorous defeat on the sea by the Republic of Genoa in the very famous battle of Meloria (1284).

Of minor turistic interest are the Palace of «Collegio Puteano» of the 17th century and the Palace of the Council of the Order (Francavilla 1603), then seat of the Law-Court of St. Stephens' Order and today seat of the High School for applied sciences «A. Pacinotti».

1. Inside of the Church of S. Stefano dei Cavalieri; 2. Piazza dei Cavalieri (Knight's Square): Palazzo della Gherardesca with the Torre della Musa.

CHURCH OF SANTA MARIA DELLA SPINA

This jewel of Gothic art of Pisan-style is located on the Lungarno Gambacorti. Initially it was an oratory at the extreme limit of the Arno River. After it was enlarged by Lupo Capomaestro in 1323 and named Chiesa della Spina (church of the thorn) because it preserved one of the thorns of the Christ crown. In the year 1871, after about five hundred years, the church was dismantled piece by piece and rebuilt in a safer location away from the river waters that had badly damaged it. This very beautiful small church is covered with an extremely rich marble decorations of gentle contrasting colours and a suggestive series of cusps and pinnacles. In the façade with three cusps there are two wooden, inlaid gates. A very fine «Madonna with Infant and Angels» of G. DI BALDUCCIO is located in an aedicule in the centre. Other aedicules are located above with statues of the school of Giovanni Pisano. Also of the school of Giovanni Pisano are the other aedicules to the right of the church with statues of the Redeemer and of the Apostles, while the statues located on the spires of the aedicules of this side are a work of NINO PISANO and his pupils.

THE INSIDE is with a nave divided by three arcades on pillars and by the presbitery. Here are works of Tommaso, son of Andrea Pisano: a Madonna with Infant and statue of St. Peter and St. John the Baptist. The «Madonna weaning her Child» of Nino Pisano together with the bas-relief of A.F. Guardi are no longer preserved in this church but in the National Museum: they are precious works of art.

CHURCH OF S. PAOLO A RIPA D'ARNO

After having visited the Chiesa della Spina, it is convenient to go to the Church of S. Paolo a Ripa d'Arno, because it is very close. It is one of the

1. A view on the «lungarno»; 2. Church of S. Maria della Spina; 3. Church of S. Paolo a Ripa d'Arno.

oldest churches of Pisa so much so that it was called «The old cathedral». It was built in the square bearing the same name in the ninth century for the Vallombrosani. Many times restored and in the eleventh and twelfth centuries submitted to many renovations. The façade and the left side are of the Gothic-Pisa Style and clearly demonstrate the same structures and decorations as later were developed in the cathedral of Piazza dei Miracoli. That is a series of blind arcades, three gates corresponding to the three inner aisles and to the three open galleries with columns, some of which are spiraled. In the arcade of the central gate there are two pendentives representing a Madonna inspired by Byzantine style (left) and one of Pisan style (right).

The Inside designed in the form of an Egyptian cross, is with three aisles, opened by a transept. Where the arms cross rises the hemisferic dome. In the two aperture windows of the apse there is an old glass window of the 14th century representing the Redeemer and nine Apostles. A Roman sarcophagus with leonine heads which served as a tomb for the jurist Burgundio in 1194, is located to the right, in the wall. This church was severely damaged during a bombing raid of the 2nd World War.

The Chapel of St. Agatha is near the church of S. Paolo a Ripa D'Arno. It is a Romanesque work, may be of DIOTISALVI, the great architect who built the Baptistry. It has an octagonal base with a pyramid shaped dome. Observe the three-mullioned windows on the faces of the octagon.

1

gallery is a big circular rose-window (rebuilt). The bell-tower of the church is made of bricks with pyramid shaped cusp and windows with two and three lights; it is perhaps a work of Giovanni di Simone but it is today of recent rehovation.

On the Inside is one nave. We see on the left wall a fine sarcophagus of the archbishop Simone Saltarelli, work of Nino and Andrea Pisano. This sarcophagus supports a triptych-aedicula. We can see, through the small columns and decorations, the lid with the prone

CHURCH OF SANTA CATERINA

It is in the square Martiri della Libertà (Martyrs for Freedom), not far from the Cathedral, in the zone of Porta a Lucca. It was built by the Dominican monks in the second half of the 13th century. The façade presents three arcades and in the middle is a gate. On the upper side there is a beautiful Gothic two orders colonnade. In the middle of the second order of the open

1. Chapel of S. Agata; 2. Church of S. Caterina.

2

statue of the late archbishop.

In the right wall we find another tombal monument, dedicated to Gherardo Compagni. This work is of the Pisa-school (14th century). On the pillars, flanking the high altar, there are two statues of Nino Pisano: the Archangel and our Lady of the Annunciation. Under the altar there is a Roman sarcophagus with the remains of the Blessed Giovanni da Rivalto.

In this church there was a very beautiful polyptych of SIMONE MARTINI, which can be admired in the National Museum. On the left wall were «The Apotheosis of St. Martin», painting of TRAINI and «The Martyrdom of St. Cecily», painting of Riminaldi. These works of the 14th century, still under renovation, are very important, and soon they should be deposed in their original places.

CHURCH OF S. FRANCESCO

It is located in the square of the same name. It was built at the beginning of the 12th century. It is a brick-building of Gothic style with the marble façade remade in 1603. The Gothic bell tower, a work of Giovanni di Simone, is of bricks with windows with two and three lights.

The Inside is in the form of an Egyptian-cross with a single nave and trussed ceiling. On the right and left walls, there are respectively five altars with paintings of different authors, such as G.B. Paggi, Passignano, F. Vanni, V. Salimbeni.

The high altar has a great polyptych of Tommaso Pisano. This marble work represents the «Madonna with Infant and Saints». The frescoes on the vault are of Taddeo Gaddi. Other remains of frescoes of the 14th century are in the chapels. On one side of the high altar, in a chapel on the right, are the bones of Count Ugolino della Gherardesca, of his sons and nephews. In the other chapels are the bones of other renowned families of Pisa. To be seen in this church is also the chapel of St. Philomela which opens out in the right wall, just before the transept, where, besides the beautiful and high Gothic vault, there is a great funeral monument of the year 1400 of the Counts Bacciamei Maggiolini, the work is of Antonio di Cheliño.

On the floor, tombal slabs and stones of different ages are numerous.

CHURCH OF SANTO SEPOLCRO

This Romanesque church, with an octagonal base, built in 1153 by the architect DIOTISALVI, is located in the homonimous square by the Lungarno. A bust of the builder, i. e. Diotisalvi, is in the lunette above the central gate. This bust is of Varni. The bell tower of the church, unfinished, is a work of the

1

same Diotisalvi. This temple was built for receiving and preserving the relics of the Holy Sepulchre (for this reason the name) brought from Jerusalem. Inside, we admire the suggestive simplicity of the temple due to the concentric architectural effect of the whole church on the high altar and just at the foot of the latter, the tomb of Maria Mancini Colonna, nephew of Mazzarino and mistress of Louis XIV.

THE OTHER PRINCIPAL CHURCHES OF PISA

Santa Cecilia. In Via Santa Cecilia, founded in 1103. The outside is like the original while the inside was renovat-

ed in the 12th century. On the high altar there is a painting of V. Salimbeni representing «The Martyrdom of St. Cecily». Here was also a bas-relief of Nino Pisano which now is in the National Museum of St. Matthew.

St. Frediano. Is in the homonimous square and is of the 11th century. The church was founded by the family Buzzacherini Sismondi. The façade is Romanesque of Pisa-Lucca Style. The ample inside, with three aisles, was rebuilt after the fire of the year 1675. Of this primitive temple are visible only the columns and pillars. The church houses a valuable painting of A. Lomi representing the «Adoration of the Wise Kings» and other paintings of V. Salimbeni. There are also frescoes of R. Manetti and D. Passignano.

Santa Maria del Carmine. Is of the year 1380 and is situated in the homonimous square. The inside with baroque altars has works of Boscoli, Lomi, Allori. From this church Napoleon ordered to remove a polyptych of Masaccio (1426).

---

1. Church of the Holy Sepulchre; 2. Church of S. Frediano.

1

The church is nearly intact in its original Romanesque form. It was founded by the «Lateranensi» around 1070. The inside of this banked church — because of the crypt below — has three aisles and antique Romanesque-Byzantine frescoes recently restored.

St. Andrea Forisportam. Was founded in the year 1100. It is situated in Via G. Giusti. Its façade, in the inferior part, is Romanesque with blind arcades. Three gates. In the upper side there is a very beautiful rose-window of Lombard type. The inside with three aisles has been altered, nevertheless the Romanesque columns with their beautiful inlaid capitals are intact as well as the whole architectural structure. In an altar to the right there is the «Holy Family» a painting of A. Lomi of the 15th century.

Dei Cappuccini. Is situated in Via dei Cappuccini, founded in the year 1200. It was the abbey of the Benedictines and dedicated to St. Donnino. In the year 1569 it was given to the Capuchins. This church was completely destroyed during the 2nd World War. The building we see today is, therefore, a recent reconstruction. In the inside there are, nevertheless, modern works of a certain importance as well as a painting of the 17th century, frescoes of the 14th century of Pisa school and a wooden crucifix of the school of Giovanni Pisano.

Santa Cristina. Is located in the Lungarno Gambacorti. It was founded in the 11th century. It is a Romanesque church with one cusp. In the inside there is the copy of the crucifix on a panel in front of which St. Catherine of Siena became the stigmata. A painting of Passignano inspired by the same episode of the stigmata is in the presbytery. This church, though transformed in recent years, shows the elegant proportions of the original construction.

St. Michele degli Scalzi. Is situated in the homonimous street by the Arno River. It is a Romanesque church of the 11th century. The façade is original only in the lower part on which are five blind arcades and three gates corresponding to the inner aisles. Because of the restoration works due to war damages and the flooding of the Arno

St. Martino. Is located in Piazza St. Martino. It is of the year 1330 and has a gate with lunette and the copy of the bas-relief titled «St. Martin and the Poor Man» of Nino Pisano.

The original work of this bas-relief is in the inside of the same church which preserves, among other things, frescoes of the Pisa school of the 14th century. It has also other frescoes of the Venetian school of the 14th century besides works of O. Riminaldi and D. Passignano. Here also are the remains of ST. BONA.

St. Michele in Borgo. Is situated in Borgo Stretto, old street of Pisa, beyond Piazza Garibaldi. It is a church of the 10th century built on the remains of a heathen temple. The façade is of the 14th century with Gothic arcades and three orders of galleries. The inside is with three aisles. The works of art here preserved are, among others, a marble crucifix of the 14th century (School of G. Pisano). On the high altar «Madonna and Saints» of B. Lomi. The triptych of the right aisle is of Taddeo di Bartolo.

St. Pierino (S. Pietro in Vinculis). Is situated in Piazza Cairoli at the beginning of Via Cavour. The square which was called «Piazza della Berlina» (Pillory Square) is one of the oldest of Pisa.

River in the year 1947, some works have been removed, such as frescoes of the Pisa school of the 11th century and other works. Observe the bell-tower with single light windows, notably inclined; this is of Romanesque style and with square base.

St. Nicola. Is in Via S. Maria, almost facing the Arno River. It is of the 12th century, but altered in the 16th and 18th centuries, with the addition of a four blind-arcades façade. The bell-tower is lightly inclined and also the inside can be visited by climbing a very interesting spiral staircase with the steps circularly disposed. The inside of the church, with its unique nave, houses paintings of the 17th century located in different chapels, and wooden sculptures of the 14th century, Pisan School.

St. Sisto. Is of the year 1073 with façade of Verrucano and tuff, pataere-decorations and majolica bowls of the 12th century. Inside there are three naves, the major of which incorporates itself semicircularly with the ancient church of St. Rocco. Antique columns and capitals, truss ceiling, two altars of the 16th century, tombstones, a panel of an unknown artist of the 14th century, antique bas-relief with Arabian verses of the Koran.

1. Church of S. Martino; 2. Church of S. Sisto; 3. Church of S. Michele in Borgo.

1

VISIT TO THE TOWN WITH A GENERAL VIEW ON THE LUNGARNI (ALONG THE RIVER) - PALACES AND FESTIVALS

Even if antique squares, monuments, palaces, gates and towers worth visiting are numerous and scattered everywhere over this town, of the more than ancient and glorious artistic and cultural traditions, we will limit ourselves to a general touristic glance. Up to now we have considered works of major renown and cultural interest just for a very short visit. We can now add, still briefly, something about the marvellous «Lungarni», and some historical and artistic elements about what the tourist may like to visit in a brief time.

We will start from:

Ponte di Mezzo. It is a bridge in the traditional centre of the town beyond Piazza Garibaldi. It was built for the first time by the Romans and has been the only bridge across the Arno River up till 1182. Later it was rebuilt many times and again destroyed during the last war. On this bridge a game takes place called the «Gioco del Ponte». From here, we can enjoy a splendid view enriched by the medieval palaces which, on the opposite banks of the river, are reflected in the water. Starting from Piazza Garibaldi, across the Ponte di Mezzo, towards the right is the GAMBACORTI PALACE of the 14th century, now seat of some municipal administrative offices. This building is of Gothic-Pisa style, three stories high with a beautiful façade, mullioned windows with two lights, marble Corinthian columns and with three-lobe small arcades. It was built by Pietro Gambacorti who ruled the town. In the inside there is a hall called of the «Baleari» with frescoes of Melani, Fardella, Salimbeni (16th and 17th centuries).

1. A view on the «lungarno»; 2. Piazza Garibaldi and Ponte di Mezzo.

Another beautiful palace along the Lungarno is the AGOSTINI PALACE of the beginning of the 15th century, decorated with terra-cotta ornaments. This building is all the more interesting as it is the only one remaining in Pisa that demonstrates the architecture of buildings of Pisa decorated with reliefs. Here is also the CAFFÈ DELL'USSERO now renovated: it was the meeting-place of many patriots of the Risorgimento and of poets and writers.

The Medici Palace, now seat of the Prefecture, is located in Piazza Mazzini, this one also is reflected in the Arno River. It was built in the 13th century and remade in the 14th century belonging at first to the D'Appiano Family then to the Medici from the 15th century. It was also the dwelling of Lorenzo il Magnifico. On the beautiful façade there are two and three decorated mullioned windows.

On the Lungarno Mediceo there is another building of the 16th century:

2

the **Toscanelli Palace**. The version according to which this construction was built from a plan of Michelangiolo is not supported by the architectural conception which is evidently of an inferior level to that of the great master: today it is the seat of the State Records Office where ancient documents of Pisan history are filed. In this palace dwelt the great poet Byron in the year 1821.

The Palazzo Reale (Royal Palace) is situated on the Lungarno Pacinotti. It is a work of 1559 of Bendinelli who realized it for Cosimo I de' Medici. Besides the Medici family the Lorena fa-

1. Palazzo Gambacorti; 2. Palazzo della Giornata; 3. Palazzo Toscanelli; 4. Palazzo Agostini.

mily dwelt here. Vittorio Emanuele the 2nd King of Italy also lived here for some time. Now it is the seat of the Monuments Supervisor Office.

The Corsini Palace together with the Scotto Garden is on the Lungarno Galilei. It's a work of the 19th century and was the residence of Shelley in the years 1821-22. It was badly damaged during the last war. In the Scotto Garden there is an open air theatre, closed off towards Piazza Guerrazzi by the Rampart of Sangallo.

1

2

3

La Cittadella vecchia (old Stronghold). From the Lungarno that runs alongside the church of St. Paolo a Ripa d'Arno and the homonimous place, we can admire the ancient Pisa-Fortress that is reflected in river waters. A wonderful sunset can be admired on this background when the sky is scattered with clouds tinged with different hues by the setting sun. This fortress of the old city was rebuilt and enlarged by Florentines who conquered Pisa in the 15th century. In 1588, Ferdinando I de' Medici built a ship-yard for the construction of galleys of St. Stephen Order. It was heavily damaged in 1944 by the rage of the war.

Illuminations of St. Ranieri. Take place every year on the evening of the 16th June along the Lungarni. For this occasion also the Leaning Tower is illuminated. It is a phantasmagoric candlelight-illumination of the beautiful medieval palaces along the Lungarni, that so lighted reproduced fantastic reflections in the waters of the river, where at the same time hundreds of flickering lights slowly float down towards the sea. This sight, which draws thousands of the town-inhabi-

tants and tourists, is crowned by an interesting fireworks display. This spectacle is in honour of the patron Saint of the town, whose feast-day recurs the day after, on the 17th of June.

1. Piazza della Berlina; 2. The Old Citadel and the bridge on the river Arno; 3. Illuminations along the Arno; 4. Torre del Campano.

4

THE HISTORICAL REGATTA AND FOLKLORE

Historical Regatta of St. Ranieri. Occurs the 17th June, feast of the Patron Saint of the town, in the Arno River with crews in costume manning antique style boats. People representing four quarters of the town take part in this game.

Gioco del Ponte (Game of the Bridge). Is a historic commemoration in costume on the Lungarno. It takes place the last Sunday of June between

opposite factions «Tramontana» (North) and «Mezzogiorno» (South), according to the natural division of the town by the river Arno. Formerly this game was called «Gioco del Mazzascudo» (Game of club and shield) and was formally disputed in Piazza dei Cavalieri (Knights' Square) in that time named «Piazza degli Anziani» (Elders's Square). Since 1490 the «Gioco del Mazzascudo» changed its name in «Gioco del Ponte» (Game of the Bridge) and takes place on the Ponte di Mezzo (Central Bridge). Before the battle that consists of pushing a trolley on rails fitted on the bridge towards the opposite bank, there is a magnificent procession along the Lungarni, with flags, insignia, tapestries. This procession is very interesting especially because of the historic commemoration realized with luxurious costumes of 16th century. Its participants are numerous citizens supporting one of the two opposite banks.

Regatta of the ancient Marine Republics. This takes place each year in June, in one of the four ancient Marine Republics: Pisa, and alternately Genoa, Amalfi and Venice.

It is a competition in the Arno River (when the regatta takes place at Pisa), between the four opposing crews all in costume and on boats of that time. Before this regatta on the river it is certainly more interesting and spectacular to see the magnificent procession executed in costumes made from models of those days. In this procession are represented Kinzica de' Sismondi (a heroine of Pisa who saved the town from the Saracens) riding a white horse; the Duke of Amalfi, Guglielmo Embriaco of Genoa called Testa di Maglio, the Doge of Venice and Caterina Cornaro. Around all these personages there are armigers and captains, page-boys and damsels.

Folklore and historic Regatta.

NATIONAL MUSEUM OF S. MATTEO

National Museum of S. Matteo (Lungarno Mediceo). The National Museum of Pisa can be rightly considered one of the most important in Europe especially for its collection of medieval and Renaissance paintings. About the sculptures either in wood, stone or marble many of them are certainly unique.

If at the beginning the aim of this gallery was to collect the works of the local art of said flourishing period, it is to be considered that this aim was largely surpassed, because neither their seat can be considered definitive (after the various movements of the works collected piece by piece through the centuries), nor can the rooms be considered sufficient because the continous affluence of works, while others can be removed for reestablishing in their original places. The Museum has today its seat in an architectural complex that was initially a Benedictine nunnery, then respectively town-jail and military barraks. As a consequence of all this,

its original structure was progressively transformed and in 1945 new restoration works was started for receiving the works of art from november 1949 on.

Entrance hall. Here we find a very beautiful «Sarcophagus of Palaeochristian art» with a picture of the «Good

1. Church of S. Matteo seat of the National Museum and Palazzo Medici seat of the Prefecture; 2. Museum: room of the dancing figures by G. Pisano. At page 76-77 Cloister inside the Museum of S. Matteo.

Shepherd», a sibyl of Giovanni Pisano, which comes from the external decoration of the Baptistry, two sculptures of the 17th century, «Endymion with a dog» and a «Venus».

FIRST ROOM. Two fragments of frescoes from the church «S. Michele degli Scalzi», fragment of Roman pillar (3rd century), a head of Tiberius.

SECOND ROOM. Various architectural fragments.

THIRD ROOM. A «Christ giving his blessing». A high-relief dated 1204 of Byzantine inspiration. A stoup of 12th century (Pisa-school), «Angel with Rose» of Biduino.

FOURTH ROOM. Marble lectern, a work of Nicola Pisano school, 13th century. An interesting «Tetramorphous with animals' heads». Three fragments of frescoes of the 14th century.

FIFTH ROOM. Practically dedicated to the Pisa-sculpture of 14th century represented by the admirable art of Giovanni Pisano.

SIXTH ROOM. Here are other sculptures of the 13th century. There is a «Madonna with Infant» detached fresco.

SEVENTH ROOM. Here are fragments of a dismantled pulpit of the church of S. Michele in Borgo (school of Giovanni Pisano). Furthermore a wooden sculpture of an artist of Lucca of the 13th century and a «Madonna with Infant» of the year 1380 (school of Nino Pisano).

EIGHT ROOM. There is a rich collection of wooden sculptures of notable importance: «The Annunciation of Mary» of Andrea Pisano, an «Annunciating Angel and an Annunciation» almost certainly of Nino, son and pupil of Andrea Pisano. There is also a very valuable «Crucifix» on panel, work of Giunta Pisano, 13th century.

NINTH ROOM. Exemplars of Medici's tapestries, a jewel box of Medici, a cabinet in walnut (executed from a sketch of Vasari). A plan of Pisa of leather.

Museum of S. Matteo. *1. The Angel of the Annunciation, polychromatic wooden sculpture; 2. Our Lady of the Annunciation, polychromatic wooden sculpture by Antonio Pisano.*

TENTH ROOM. Is dedicated to the paintings of the 15th and 16th centuries: «Redeemer with Angels» of Ambrogio d'Asti, a «Pietà» of Jacopo del Sellaio, «St. Eulalia from Barcelona» (unknown artist of 15th century), «St. Jerome» of a German artist, 15th century.

ELEVENTH ROOM. Here also are sculptures, predominantly in wood. On the empty pedestal there was the famous bust of St. Lussorio, work of Donatello, given back to the Chiesa dei Cavalieri. «Bust of the Redeemer» terra-cotta of Verrocchio. A beautiful crib of Della Robbia. A «Virgin praying», school of Della Robbia. Wooden «crucifix» of a Catalan artist of the 15th century.

TWELFTH ROOM. Precious exemplars of ancient painting; parchment papers and miniatures of the 13th century.

THIRTEENTH ROOM. «The Virgin» of Giovanni Pisano, work of great value. There is a marble piece of Tino da Camaino. A precious «crucifix» in rock crystal of the 13th century. Fragments of Barbaresque tombs found in the excavations of the Cathedral square.

FOURTEENTH ROOM. Paintings of Sogliani, Pacchiarotti, Ambrogio d'Asti.

FIFTEENTH ROOM. Small wooden model of the Chiesa dei Cavalieri (church of the knights), attributed to Giovanni de' Medici and Bontalenti. Paintings of Ciafferi. Drawing of the 17th century «Queen of Sheba visiting Solomon».

SIXTEENTH ROOM. «Model» in plaster of the inside of the Chiesa dei Cavalieri (Church of the Knights), of Poccianti 1855.

SEVENTEENTH ROOM. There are paintings of Lomi. A «St. Francis» attributed to Correggio or to Cigoli. A great painting depicting the «Sacred and profane Love» of Guido Reni.

EIGHTEENTH ROOM. Model of the church of S. Stefano dei Cavalieri (St. Stephen of the knights). Collection of paintings of artists of the 18th century.

NINETEENTH ROOM. Recently prepared and dedicated to old coins. This room is located in the Ancient Capitulary Hall. The medal show-case is very precious and exceptionally important.
On the second storey are:

TWENTIETH ROOM. The most striking work is undoubtedly the great altarpiece «Madonna with Infant» and flanking it «The histories of the Master of St. Martin» a masterpiece of Pisa painting of the 13th century. There are furthermore two crosses (Pisa painting) with scenes painted on golden background «Living Christ» and «Suffering Christ». Various distempers on panel of the 13th century.

TWENTY-FIRST ROOM. Here is kept the very famous polyptych of Simone Martini «Madonna, St. Catherine and Saints». This work comes from the Church of St. Catherine. Then, there is one of the most beautiful masterpieces of Nino Pisano, the «Madonna nursing her Child» (14th century). Furthermore other works, among which distempers on panels, of the 14th century and figures of St. John and St. Paul (Master of St. Torpé).

TWENTY-SECOND ROOM. Here are works of the Pisa-school of the 14th century with artists of Pisa and Siena, such as Giovanni di Nicola, B. Falconi, Turino Vanni. There is also a «Crucifixion» of Cecco di Pietro and the «Histories of the Life of St. Galgano» (unknown author).

TWENTY-THIRD ROOM. Can be called the room of the tapestries hung on the walls: «Roman Consul receiving gifts» (Flemish school of the 18th century), «Clement VII receiving a Cardinal» (Florentine school of the 16th century), «Giovanni de' Medici Encouraging the Arts» (Florentine school, 16th century), «Cosimo I de' Medici received by Pius IV», «Sacrifice» (Flemish school, 17th century), «David presented to Saul» (Florentine school, 16th century), «The Faith» (Florentine school, 17th century), «Bear-Hunt» (Workshop of Gobelins, 16th century), «The Charity» (Florentine school, 17th century). In the show-cases there are valuable illuminated books of anthems of artists of Pisa and Siena of the 13th and 14th centuries.

TWENTY-FOURTH ROOM. The room of major interest, where many important works, real masterpieces, are shown: «St. Paul» of Masaccio, «Madonna with Infant» of Gentile da Fabriano, «Madonna of Humility» (Master of Città di Castello), «Madon-

1

2

3

1. Madonna and Child and histories, by the Maestro di S. Martino; 2. Madonna and Child and histories, detail; 3. Crucifix by Giunta Pisano.

na with Jesus and donors» of Benozzo Gozzoli.

TWENTY-FIFTH ROOM. Paintings on panels of Giovanni di Pietro, Spinello Aretino, Turino Vanni.

TWENTY-SIXTH ROOM. Here are works of Taddeo di Bartolo and his school. There are also works of the Pisa school of the 14th century.

TWENTY-SEVENTH ROOM. A procession roller-towel depicting the Crucifixion and Scourging. Then an «Annunciation» of Giovanni da Milano. Other paintings of secondary importance.

TWENTY-EIGHT ROOM. Tuscan painting of the 14th century.

TWENTY-NINTH ROOM. Other paintings. Here are Paolo Schiavo, Raffaellino del Garbo «Madonna with Infant and Saints». Other paintings of Neri, Bicci, Macchiavelli.

THIRTIETH ROOM. «St. Sebastian and St. Rocco» of Ghirlandaio, «Canephora», frescoed fragment of Ghirlandaio, «St. Christopher» of Giani.

THIRTY-FIRST ROOM. Two panels with «Madonna, Infant and Saints» of

1

Ghirlandaio, «Martyrdom of St. Sebastian» of B. della Gatta.

THIRTY-SECOND ROOM. Paintings of Florentine school of the 15th century.

Three sides of a chest (fragments) with «Scenes of a Battle» (Arts master of the family Adimari).

THIRTY-THIRD ROOM. «Rebecca and Eliazar standing by a well» opera of Rosso Fiorentino. «The Holy Family» of Pierin del Vaga, «Madonna with Infant and Saints» of Domenico Puligo. Painted copies of Tuscan mannerists.

THIRTY-FOURTH ROOM. Collection of paintings and panels (Florentine artists of the 16th century). «St. Francis dying» of A. Sogliani, «St. Anthony in the grotta» of A. Boscoli.

1. Polyptic of the Madonna and Child with Saints by Simone Martini (1320).

THIRTY-FIFTH ROOM. Very interesting works of the Ceci-Donation comprising Italian artists of the 17th and 18th century, among which: Tempesti, Strozzi, G.M. Crespi, with the interesting opera «Pulce» (flea). Moreover: Magnaschi, V. Castello, Gagliani, B. Castiglione.

THIRTY-SIXTH ROOM. Collection of marble mirrors carved by A. Guardi in the year 1462 for a church of Pisa.

1. Madonna del Latte by Nino Pisano; 2. S. Paolo by Masaccio (1426).

1

THIRTY-SEVENTH ROOM. Here are preserved foreign paintings. A long series of landscapes, portraits, etc. The «St. Catherine of Alexandria» of a Flemish artist, 18th century, is one of the most valuable works together with «Our Lady of the Sorrows» of the French school, 16th century. Works of Jean and Pietro Brueghel. Portraits of Winterhalter, Le Brun, Lawrence terminate the series of works of this interesting room.

1. Room of the tapestries: illuminated codex; 2. Madonna and Child by Gentile da Fabriano.

2

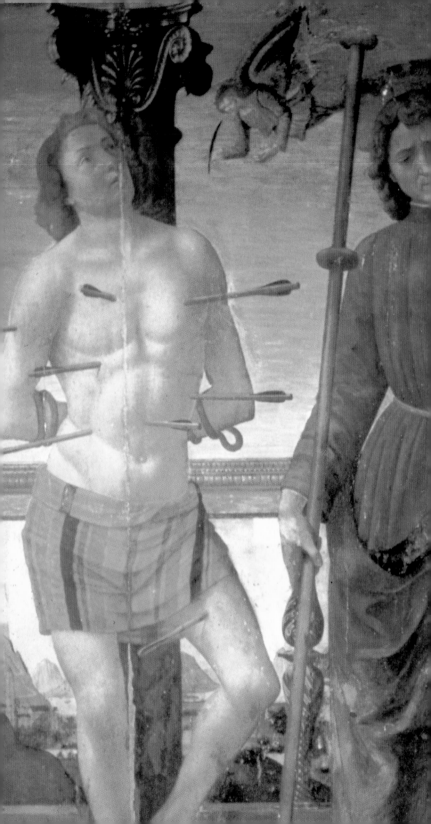

UNIVERSITY

Situated in Via XXIX Maggio in a building of the 15th century of a scarce architectural value, the façade of which has been recently rebuilt.

The institution of the «Sapienza» goes back to very remote times, it is one of the most glorious and ancient among the Italian universities. Today in this university all the faculties are represented. It has a very rich library comprising interesting scientific collections and original documents, partly written by Galileo Galilei himself. To the University is annexed also a Museum of Natural History and the Botanic Garden.

1. S. Sebastiano and S. Rocco by Domenico Ghirlandaio; 2. Monument inside the University courtyard; 3. The University courtyard.

2

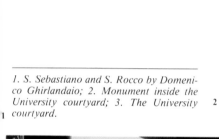

1

3

University of Pisa: *1. The historic «aula Magna» (Assembly Hall); 2. The botanical gardens; 3. The Carthusian Monastery of Pisa.*

TOURS OF THE SURROUNDINGS OF PISA

From Pisa, located near to other great centres such as Lucca, 18 kms, Leghorn, 20 kms and Viareggio, 20 kms, numerous touristic, historical and cultural spots can be easily and quickly reached by road, highway or rail. Among the most interesting cities and spots, to be visited in the arc of a day or even in a few hours are the following: LUCCA, LIVORNO, VIAREGGIO with the Versilia Riviera up to Massa-Carrara and Marble Quarries in the Apuanian Alps. Furthermore the beaches of Marina di Pisa with the estuary of the Arno and Tirrenia. The Massaciuccoli Lake with the country-house of Giacomo Puccini (Village of Torre del Lago Puccini). The Carthusian Monastery of Pisa located in the commune of Calci. The Basilica of S. Piero a Grado, S. Giuliano Terme, etc.

The Carthusian Monastery of Pisa (Calci). 13 kms from Pisa. It rises in a fertile country among the valleys with olive-trees and vineyards where peace and silence absolute reign. It was founded in the year 1366 and comprises church, cloisters, cells of the Carthusians and guest-rooms. Many are the works of a certain artistic importance and interest but the visitor will be mostly impressed by the charm due to the late-baroque style of the white buildings rich in marbles contrasting with the green of the surrounding countryside to create an atmosphere of elegance and at the same time a sensation of religiousness most appropriate to the setting. The tourist, after his visit to the Carthusian Monastery of Pisa, should not omit a visit to the PARISH CHURCH of CALCI, romanesque art, founded at the end of the 11th century with its urn inside the high-altar containing the relics of Saint Ermolao, Patron Saint of the valley. The remains were placed in this church in the year 1111 by the Archbishop of Pisa Pietro Moriconi.

Romanesque Basilica of S. Pietro a Grado (7 kms from Pisa) on the road to the sea, leading to Tirrenia. The origin of this ancient basilica is tied to a legend. In the 1880 Da Morrona wrote: «St. Peter arrived from Antioch and when landing along the Tuscan shore, in a place called Grado (step), so named because of the steps, washed by the waves, where the boats landed, judged it an appropriate place for rising the first altar and temporarily founding a church». During recent excavations in fact, an ancient church of the 6th cen-

tury was discovered located under the present one which was constructed in the 12th century.

The work is of Romanesque style, presents four apses and is made of tuff. The inside, with its three aisles, has frescoes of the 13th century and the portraits of the Popes, starting from St. Peter up to Giovanni XVII. Inside it resembles the Palaeochristian basilicas.

Country-House of Giacomo Puccini. Lies beside the lake of Massaciuccoli near the centre of Torre del Lago,

12 kms approximately from Pisa on the road to Viareggio and the Versilian Riviera. Inside the country-house of the great musician of Lucca there are his piano, personal belongings and hunting-equipment, family tomb, objects of art. In the large square in front of the lake we can see the statue of the master. There are also typical restaurants. There is a service of motor-boats for touring the picturesque lake which has the hills of Massarosa and Apuan Alps as a background.

PLEASANT SPOTS ON THE OUTSKIRTS OF PISA

During a stay at Pisa one cannot miss the visit of S. GIULIANO TERME at 6 kms from the town, a charming ther-mal resort at the foot of Pisa mountains. Its waters are of a millenary renown. An interesting view of Pisa with its monuments can be enjoyed travelling along the bends of the National Brennero road towards Lucca.

There are other localities such as **Rigoli, Molina di Quosa, Pugnano, Ripafratta** where we can see the Romanesque Parish churches of the 12th-13th century and the villas and gardens of the families Agostini, Roncioni, Dal Borgo, ancient towers and castles scattered in fertile vineyards and

1. The Romanesque Basilica of S. Piero a Grado; 2. Inside of the Basilica: fresco on the aisle wall (detail); 3. Interior, excavations of the old 6th century church; 4. Villa Puccini; 5. S. Giuliano Terme.

olive groves.

Cascina is 13 kms from Pisa, a centre of wood-carving with a permanent exhibition of furniture. This little town has also a very famous Parish church.

S. Miniato is 40 kms away, a little town founded on the top of three hills from where one can enjoy a vast view of the Arno low lands, the Pistoia and Florentine Mountains and, on the other side, the wavering succession of high-land that from the zone of Volterra slowly declines towards the shores of the Tyrrhenian Sea. A visit to the numerous works of art scattered everywhere in this charming town should not be missed.

65 kms away is **Volterra**, a centre of historic and artistic importance with its monuments of ancient Etruscan and Roman civilizations. Very interesting is the «Piazza dei Priori» (Priors' Square) with its Palace, the Baptistry, the Etruscan Gate and the Strongholds.

Along the avenues of the Stron-

gholds, lined with trees, one can enjoy a vast view as far as the Tyrrhenian Shore, together with charming sunsets and plays of light.

Vicopisano is 19 kms from Pisa with its very ancient fortress of the 15th century (the design is attributed to the great Brunelleschi) and with its Romanesque Parish church of the 13th century.

---

1. S. Miniato. Volterra: 1. The Tower of Palazzo Priori; 2. The crags and the Abbey; 3. Etruscan cinerary urn; 4. The Etruscan porta dell'Arco (Arch Gate).

CONTENTS

Graphics and typesetting by:
FEDERICO FRASSINETTI
Photographs by:
ASCANIO ASCANI - MISANO (FO)
LINO FRASSINETTI

editions **ITALCARDS** bologna - italy

Printed
LA FOTOMETALGRAFICA EMILIANA SPA
San Lazzaro di Savena - Bologna